DRUGS

STEROIDS AND OTHER PERFORMANCE-ENHANCING DRUGS

A MyReportLinks.com Book

David Aretha

MyReportLinks.com Books

an imprint of

Enslow Publishers, Inc.

Box 398, 40 Industrial Road
Berkeley Heights, NJ 07922
USA

MyReportLinks.com Books, an imprint of Enslow Publishers, Inc. MyReportLinks®
is a registered trademark of Enslow Publishers, Inc.

Library of Congress Cataloging-in-Publication Data

Aretha, David.
  Steroids and other performance-enhancing drugs / David Aretha.
    p. cm. — (Drugs)
  Includes bibliographical references and index.
  ISBN 0-7660-5277-X
  1. Anabolic steroids—Juvenile literature. I. Title. II. Drugs (Berkeley Heights, N.J.)
  RC1230.A74 2005
  362.29'9—dc22
                                    2004007005

Printed in the United States of America

10 9 8 7 6 5 4 3 2 1

To Our Readers:
Through the purchase of this book, you and your library gain access to the Report Links that specifically back up this book.
The Publisher will provide access to the Report Links that back up this book and will keep these Report Links up to date on **www.myreportlinks.com** for five years from the book's first publication date.
We have done our best to make sure all Internet addresses in this book were active and appropriate when we went to press. However, the author and the Publisher have no control over, and assume no liability for, the material available on those Internet sites or on other Web sites they may link to.
The usage of the MyReportLinks.com Books Web site is subject to the terms and conditions stated on the Usage Policy Statement on **www.myreportlinks.com**.
A password may be required to access the Report Links that back up this book. The password is found on the bottom of page 4 of this book.
Any comments or suggestions can be sent by e-mail to comments@myreportlinks.com or to the address on the back cover.

Photo Credits: AP/Wide World Photos, pp. 13, 18, 29; © 1995–2004 The Nemours Foundation, p. 14; © 2001–2004, Oregon Health & Science University, p. 43; © 2004 American Academy of Family Physicians, p. 20; Corbis, p. 1; Executive Office of the President/Office of National Drug Control Policy, p. 31; Food & Drug Administration, p. 41; Hemera Photo-Objects, p. 1; MyReportLinks.com Books, p. 4; National Collegiate Athletic Association, p. 21; Photos.com, p. 37; Stockbyte: Sensitive Issues, pp. 3 (handcuffed man), 35, 39; U.S. Department of Health and Human Services/The National Institute on Drug Abuse, p. 27; U.S. Department of Justice/The National Drug Intelligence Center, p. 11; U.S. Drug Enforcement Administration, pp. 3 (pills and bottle), 9, 17, 23, 25, 33;

Cover Photo: Corbis (man flexing); Hemera Photo-Objects (background).

Disclaimer: While the stories of abuse in this book are real, many of the names have been changed.

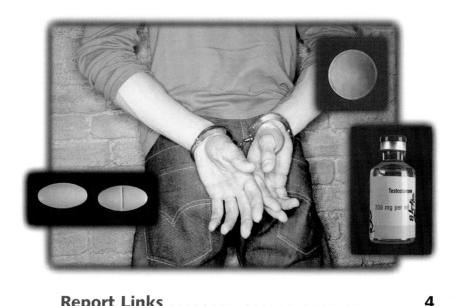

About MyReportLinks.com Books

MyReportLinks.com Books
Great Books, Great Links, Great for Research!

The Internet sites listed on the next four pages can save you hours of research time. These Internet sites—we call them "Report Links"—are constantly changing, but we keep them up to date on our Web site.

Give it a try! Type http://www.myreportlinks.com into your browser, click on the series title, then the book title, and scroll down to the Report Links listed for this book.

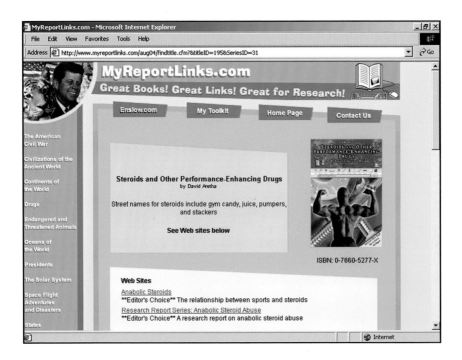

The Report Links will bring you to great source documents, photographs, and illustrations. MyReportLinks.com Books save you time, feature Report Links that are kept up to date, and make report writing easier than ever!

Please see "To Our Readers" on the copyright page for important information about this book, the MyReportLinks.com Web site, and the Report Links that back up this book.

Please enter **DRS1356** if asked for a password.

Report Links

> The Internet sites described below can be accessed at
> http://www.myreportlinks.com

▶**Anabolic Steroids**   *EDITOR'S CHOICE

This special report from ESPN provides a look at anabolic steroids and the impact they have on the world of sports.

▶**Research Report Series: Anabolic Steroid Abuse**   *EDITOR'S CHOICE

Learn what steroids are, why people use them, the scope of steroid abuse, the health consequences, and the effect these drugs have on behavior, at this Web site. Prevention and treatment are also discussed.

▶**Anabolic Steroids: NIDA for Teens**   *EDITOR'S CHOICE

Read about what anabolic steroids can do to teenagers and their bodies. Information on what steroids are and how teens use them is included.

▶**What You Should Know About Steroids**   *EDITOR'S CHOICE

This Web site from KidsHealth provides an overview of what steroids are, how they work, and the dangers of taking them.

▶**Get the Facts About Steroids**   *EDITOR'S CHOICE

Get the straight facts on steroids. Learn more about the dangers of steroid use at this Web site.

                                                       *EDITOR'S CHOICE

▶**Steroids Fast Facts**

This site from the National Drug Intelligence Center provides quick and concise answers to some of the most frequently asked questions about steroids. Learn about the risks involved in taking them, who is likely to use them, and much more.

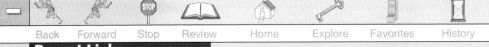
Report Links

**The Internet sites described below can be accessed at
http://www.myreportlinks.com**

▶Anabolic Steroid Abuse

A collection of current information on steroid abuse is available at this site. The articles that are provided discuss how people can help stop this growing problem.

▶Anabolic Steroids?

This online research paper from Duke University examines the scope of anabolic steroid use, the health consequences of their use, their effects on behavior, their addictiveness, treatment programs, and more.

▶Anabolic Steroids: National Library of Medicine

The National Institutes of Health provides general overviews on steroids as well as research papers, treatment possibilities, and the legal consequences of using banned substances. Links to national organizations are also included.

▶Are Steroids Worth the Risk?

Developed for teenagers, this fact sheet explains what steroids are and how they work in the body. You will also learn about the dangers of steroids, their effects, and alternatives to using them.

▶ATHENA (Athletes Targeting Healthy Exercise & Nutrition Alternatives)

The ATHENA program is designed to teach young women about positive body image, exercise, and healthy nutrition in the hopes of reducing eating disorders. Emphasis is also placed on reducing the number of athletes who use diet pills.

▶ATLAS (Athletes Training & Learning to Avoid Steroids)

Learn about ATLAS, a steroid drug prevention program designed to help promote healthy nutrition and exercise as an alternative to drug use for male high school athletes. You will learn about the dangers of steroid use.

▶Basic Facts About Drugs: Steroids

Developed for young people, this fact sheet explains what steroids are and the different methods of their use. It also provides information on signs of steroid use and short- and long-term consequences.

▶Black Market Anabolic Steroids

Steroids are illegal, and possessing them can get you in trouble with the law unless you have a legitimate prescription from a physician. Learn about the consequences of buying steroids from black-market sources.

Report Links

The Internet sites described below can be accessed at
http://www.myreportlinks.com

▶ Canadian Centre for Ethics in Sports (CCES)

The Canadian Centre for Ethics in Sports is a nonprofit organization
that promotes fair play programs internationally. Learn more about fair
play and drug-free sports activities at the CCES Web site.

▶ Do You Know What Your Sports Supplement Is?

Anabolic steroids are not the only substances that athletes use to enhance their
performance. Find out more about energy boosters, fat burners, protein powders,
amino acids, creatine, prohormones, and others.

▶ Drug Trends: Use of Ephedrine Products

Read about ephedrine, and learn what substances contain this drug. A list of the
ill effects that have been linked to ephedrine use is included.

▶ Ergogenic Aids: Counseling the Athlete

View a detailed chart summarizing a large number of ergogenic aids, such as
anabolic steroids and caffeine. Learn more about the prices of some of these
drugs and the reported side effects of anabolic steroids.

▶ Examples of Research-Based Drug Abuse Prevention Programs

A selection of behavior modification programs are listed with contact
information. Learn the strategies you need to stay drug-free.

▶ The Healthy Competition Foundation

The Healthy Competition Foundation provides educational and research
materials on performance-enhancing drugs in the hopes of encouraging drug-
free sports competitions. Learn more about the health dangers and how you can
overcome peer pressure.

▶ Juveniles and Drugs

Learn more about the serious effects that drugs, such as steroids, have on the
health, behavior, and development of young people.

▶ NAADAC, The Association for Addiction Professionals

NAADAC focuses on eliminating drug, tobacco, alcohol, and gaming addictions
through prevention, intervention, and quality treatment. This group hopes to
create healthier families and communities. Discover more about their programs
at the NAADAC Web site.

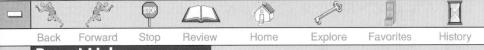
Report Links

**The Internet sites described below can be accessed at
http://www.myreportlinks.com**

▶ **The Safety and Efficacy of Anabolic Steroid Precursors:
What is the Scientific Evidence?**

This online paper outlines the risks involved with taking anabolic steroid precursors that are available in stores across the country. Learn if they work, if they are safe to take, and if the risks outweigh the benefits.

▶ **Steroids: Play Safe, Play Fair**

Steroid use can be very dangerous and is banned by most sports organizations, including the International Olympic Committee. Learn more about these performance-enhancing supplements and how they affect males and females.

▶ **Steroids: The Hard Truth**

Explore teenage steroid use through personal accounts at this PBS site. Discussion includes the realities of teen steroid use and information from medical experts.

▶ **Steroids and Sports: A Dangerous Mix?**

Find out more about the dangerous long-term effects of steroids at this Web site. Anabolic steroids, androstenedione, and creatine are all covered.

▶ **Steroids Quest**

Learn about how drugs affect your brain and body. This Web site features an interactive series of fun questions designed to teach you about steroids.

▶ **Teen Athletes and Performance-Enhancing Substances:
What Parents Can Do**

The Mayo Clinic provides parents with an informative overview of steroids and other performance-enhancing drugs. Learn why teenagers take steroids and what you can do to help them.

▶ **Tips for Teens: The Truth About Steroids**

Facts that teens should know before ever trying steroids. Some myths concerning steroids are disproven, and the information helps to give a clear picture of the risks involved in using these types of drugs.

▶ **What's up with Prescription and Over-the-Counter Drugs?**

Learn about some of the popular misconceptions of anabolic steroids. Young people talk about what they have heard.

Steroids and Other Performance-Enhancing Drugs Facts

✘ Reports state that at least a million Americans use anabolic steroids outside their intended purposes.

✘ A 2003 study reported that 2.5 percent of eighth graders and 3.5 percent of twelfth graders had abused steroids at least once in their lifetimes.

✘ The same 2003 study found that 21.7 percent of eighth graders and 40.7 percent of twelfth graders believed that steroids were "fairly easy" or "very easy" to obtain.

✘ The black market for anabolic steroids is a $400-million-a-year business.

✘ More than one hundred different types of anabolic steroids have been developed, none of which are legal in the United States without a prescription.

✘ Steroids' numerous side effects include heart attacks, strokes, cancer, and severe depression, which can lead to suicide.

✘ Male-specific side effects for steroids include prostate enlargement, shriveled testicles, breast development, reduced sperm production, and impotence.

✘ Female-specific side effects for steroids include disrupted menstrual cycles, facial hair growth, and a deepened voice.

✘ Steroids can cause stunted growth in adolescents.

✘ According to a 2001 study, a million kids ages twelve to seventeen had taken potentially dangerous performance-enhancing supplements.

✘ Studies have found that the effects of legal prohormones (such as androstenedione) seem to mimic those of anabolic steroids.

✘ In his 2004 State of the Union address, President George W. Bush urged Americans and professional athletes to stop abusing anabolic steroids and performance-

Testosterone

200 mg per ml

FRIGHTFUL STORIES

Preston Collins,* age fifteen, played high school football in Bakersfield, California. He was an honor student who had never gotten into trouble—until he discovered anabolic steroids. Preston took the drug to build up his muscles. According to his family members, though, it caused him to commit the most heinous of crimes.

In the early morning of July 3, 2001, Preston stormed into his mother's bedroom and stabbed her to death. Psychiatrists call such aggression "roid rage," one of the many ugly side effects of anabolic steroids.

"Most people I talk to—educated people—had no idea about roid rage," said Eliza Wilson, Collins paternal grandmother. "They know about cocaine abuse and marijuana and heroin. They don't know about steroids. But it's real."[1]

▶ Steroids and Performance-Enhancing Substances

Testosterone is a hormone produced abundantly in males and, to a much lesser degree, in females. Testosterone makes the body masculine and contributes to muscular development. Anabolic steroids are a lab-made version of testosterone.

Doctors sometimes use anabolic steroids to treat patients who have cancer or other illnesses. It is illegal to purchase the drug without a prescription, but millions of people have done so. They do this because the drug's anabolic effect aids in the development of muscles. Anabolic steroids help males and females increase their strength and build muscle quickly. For athletes and bodybuilders, steroids are an apparent quick fix to achieving their goals.

*While the stories of abuse in this book are real, many of the names have been changed.

Many who use the drug, however, pay a heavy price. Anabolic steroids can lead to health problems. Over time, users may experience acne, rapid weight gain, liver damage, heart attacks, and strokes. Steroids often lead to aggressive and violent behavior—roid rage—as well as extreme depression. These are just a few of the drug's frightening side effects. Despite these dangers, at least a million Americans use anabolic steroids outside their intended purposes. Hundreds of thousands of these users are teenagers.

Because anabolic steroids are so dangerous—and illegal—other performance-enhancing supplements have become popular in recent years. Prohormones (also known as prosteroids and steroid precursors) are natural supplements that are similar to steroids. These supplements, such as androstenedione, are

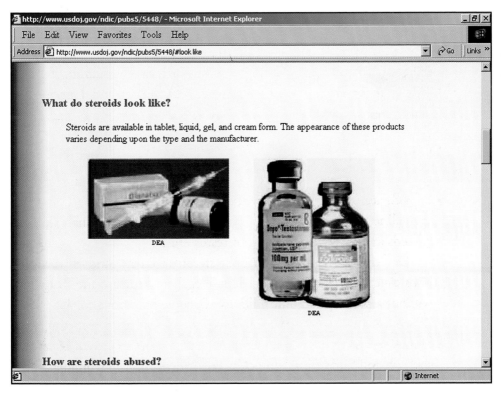

▲ Steroids are available in many different forms, including cream, gel, liquid, and tablet.

currently legal in the United States and most places. They are sold over the counter at a number of vitamin and drug stores. However, while prohormones help build muscle, they can have some side effects similar to steroids. This is among the reasons why Canada has banned androstenedione.

Falling Giants

Ray McNeil was a prominent bodybuilder, earning the title "Mr. California." He was married to Sally McNeil, a fellow body-builder. Both used steroids to gain an advantage in their careers. The McNeils argued often, and due to the effects of steroids, neither could control his or her anger. During arguments, Ray sometimes beat Sally severely.

After Ray came home late on Valentine's Day in 1995, the couple started arguing. Their wrath escalated to the point where Sally called the police, claiming her husband was beating her. Sally, too, could not control her roid rage. With her two children looking on, she pulled out a twelve-gauge shotgun and shot her husband in the stomach. She then reloaded and shot him in the face. Sally is now serving time in a maximum-security prison.

Lyle Alzado was a ferocious defensive player in the National Football League (NFL). A Pro Bowler (an NFL all-star), he led the Los Angeles Raiders to victory in the 1984 Super Bowl. Fans loved him for his manic play and bone-jarring hits. Alzado, though, consumed large doses of steroids and could not control his emotions. His teammates called him "Rainbow" because of his variety of moods—caused by steroids. The drugs eventually led to cancer, and he died at age forty-three.

"I started taking anabolic steroids in 1969 and never stopped," Alzado said just days before his death. "It was addict-ing, mentally addicting. Now I'm sick, and I'm scared. . . . I became very violent on the field and off it. I did things only crazy people do. Once a guy sideswiped my car and I beat the hell out of him. Now look at me. My hair's gone, I wobble when I walk

Lyle Alzado salutes the fans after the Raiders won Super Bowl XVIII in 1984. Alzado died a slow and painful death brought on by his steroid use. He was just forty-three years old when he died.

and have to hold on to someone for support, and I have trouble remembering things. My last wish? That no one else ever dies this way."[2]

Everyday Stories

Steroids have ruined relationships, shocked communities, and cost people their lives. Psychiatrist Harrison Pope of McLean Hospital in Massachusetts studied eighty-eight athletes who used steroids. Pope found that 23 percent of the users suffered "major mood disturbances," including mania and severe depression. Steroid users also reported aggressive or violent incidents.

Pope recounted that one steroid user, stuck in traffic, got out and smashed three cars with his fists and a metal bar. Another was

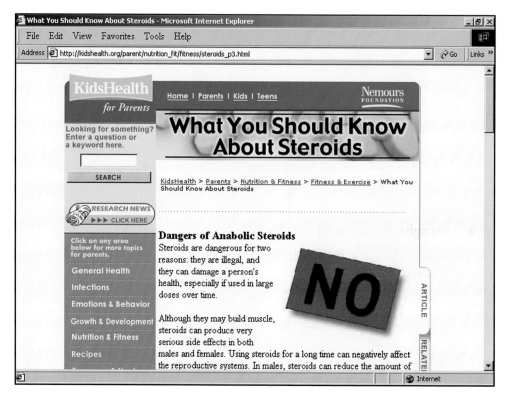

▲ The severe health-related and legal problems caused by using steroids deter most people from ever trying them.

arrested for assaulting a motorist. Another rammed his head through a wooden door. Pope reported that some of the steroid users were kicked out of their homes by their parents, wives, or girlfriends because they were intolerably aggressive.[3]

Bobby was a typical teenage athlete from Texas. As a high school football player, he admired his muscle-bound teammates. Bobby, determined to star on the field and have more confidence with girls, began taking steroids during his junior year.

By May, Bobby had packed on twenty pounds of muscle. He often stared in the mirror for up to fifteen minutes, admiring his physique. In the weight room, he increased his bench press by 125 pounds (56.7 kilograms). As a senior, he made the starting lineup and nearly made all-district.

Yet more and more, the steroids were affecting Bobby's health and mind. Sometimes, his whole body felt sore. He sweated profusely, and a rash broke out on his back. Hiding the rash (a sign of steroid abuse), Bobby did not shower at school and changed shirts quickly. As a senior, his face broke out with pimples—which he tried to cover up with makeup. When his testicles began to shrink, he started to panic.

Bobby did not like what was happening to him, but he was afraid to tell anyone his secret. He began to read everything he could on steroids. He read how they damaged the liver and the heart, led to cancer, and caused rage and depression. Scared straight, Bobby never took steroids again.[4] Just as in Bobby's case, if you or someone you know is using steroids, it is never too late to stop.

Chapter 2 ▶

HISTORY OF STEROIDS

In 1935, scientists in Amsterdam isolated a chemical from mice testes, which they identified as testosterone. Later that year, a German research team led by scientist Adolph Butenandt successfully synthesized testosterone, earning Butenandt the Nobel Prize for Chemistry. While some doctors put the new drug to good use, Adolf Hitler's doctors developed more sinister plans.

▶ The First Uses and Abuses

In the late 1930s, doctors used steroids to treat hypogonadism. With that condition, a young man's testicles do not produce enough testosterone for normal growth or for the changes that occur during puberty. Meanwhile in Nazi Germany, doctors were more interested in the drug's muscle-building effects. They were looking to pursue Hitler's dream of the masculine white male— the "Aryan Superman." The Nazis experimented with steroids first on dogs and then on German soldiers. They hoped to increase the soldiers' performance and aggressiveness on the battlefield during World War II.

After the war ended in 1945, the Allies gave anabolic steroids to underfed concentration camp survivors as a way to rebuild body tissue. Some doctors prescribed the drug to treat a variety of conditions, including impotence and anemia. However, many doctors feared that steroids' side effects, largely unknown at the time, could be severe. Some physicians even referred to the drug as "medical dynamite."[1]

Despite such fears, Soviet wrestlers and weight lifters began taking testosterone as early as the late 1940s. An American

Steroids were first developed in the 1930s. There are some legitimate medical benefits of these drugs for those who desperately need them, but use of steroids needs to be closely supervised by doctors.

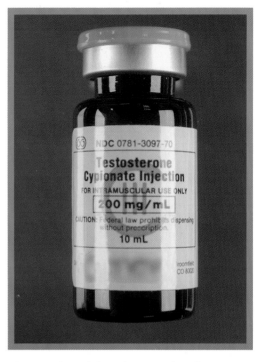

doctor named John Ziegler witnessed their success at the 1956 World Games in Moscow. He wanted to give American athletes the same edge. Soon, he developed a synthetic drug closely related to testosterone—but with fewer side effects. It was called synthetic anabolic hormone steroids. In 1958, the pharmaceutical company Ciba marketed his drug under the name Dianabol. Among athletes, Dianabol became very popular.

Companies developed more sophisticated brands of synthetic anabolic steroids. By the 1960s, the drug became very popular among weight lifters, football players, and other strength-oriented athletes. In 1975, the International Olympic Committee prohibited Olympic athletes from using anabolic steroids because it gave them an unnatural and unfair advantage.

Over time, most pro and amateur sports leagues also banned steroids, including the NFL, the National Collegiate Athletic Association (NCAA), and youth leagues. Yet anabolic steroid use still flourished throughout the 1970s and 1980s—and it was not just muscle men who were taking it. Athletes in speed-oriented sports "juiced up" because the drug helped them train harder. Moreover, amateur bodybuilders and many noncompetitive athletes also took the drug. Year after year, scientists reported the harmful side effects of steroids, but demand remained high.

▲ After the 1988 Summer Olympics, Canadian sprinter Ben Johnson was stripped of his medals and world record because he tested positive for steroids. Most major amateur and professional sports organizations have banned the use of steroids and some other performance-enhancing substances.

The biggest controversy surrounding steroids occurred at the 1988 Summer Olympics. Canada's Ben Johnson won the gold medal in the 100-meter dash. However, he was stripped of his medal after testing positive for anabolic steroids. Johnson was branded a cheater, and the story made headlines worldwide.

Soon, the United States government took a stand against the drug. Under the Anti-Drug Abuse Act of 1988, the sale of anabolic steroids for nonmedical purposes became a federal offense. In 1990, Congress increased penalties for the sale and use of the drug. Some doctors even went to prison for prescribing anabolic steroids for nonmedical purposes.

Despite the tough laws, athletes with enough persistence could buy steroids illegal or on the black market. Moreover, alternatives to steroids became available. They were about as effective (and dangerous) as anabolic steroids—but they were legal.

Emergence of Prohormones

At one time, the U.S. Food and Drug Administration (FDA) regulated dietary supplements. These supplements included vitamins, minerals, herbs, and other nutritional substances. In the early 1990s, many Americans wanted to take dietary supplements for health reasons, but they often could not buy many supplements because the FDA had not thoroughly tested and approved them. In 1994, Congress relaxed FDA regulations of supplements in its Dietary Supplement Health and Education Act.

Unfortunately, some of the newly legal supplements were steroid precursors, also called prosteroids and prohormones. Though technically natural supplements, these prohormones converted to testosterone once ingested. Thus, prohormones such as androstenedione and androstenediol could be just as effective and potentially harmful as anabolic steroids.

As legal supplements, prohormones are sold in big numbers in health food stores and on the Internet. Though such substances were banned by many sports organizations, anyone could buy

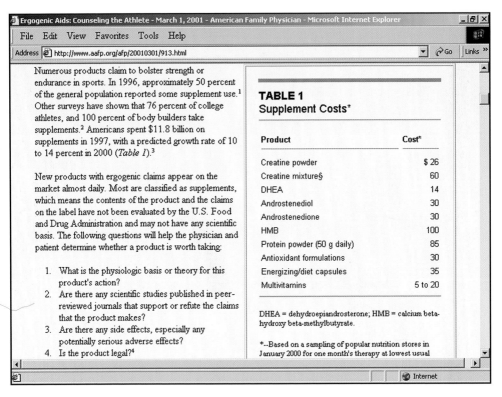

Numerous products claim to bolster strength or endurance in sports. In 1996, approximately 50 percent of the general population reported some supplement use.[1] Other surveys have shown that 76 percent of college athletes, and 100 percent of body builders take supplements.[2] Americans spent $11.8 billion on supplements in 1997, with a predicted growth rate of 10 to 14 percent in 2000 (*Table 1*).[3]

New products with ergogenic claims appear on the market almost daily. Most are classified as supplements, which means the contents of the product and the claims on the label have not been evaluated by the U.S. Food and Drug Administration and may not have any scientific basis. The following questions will help the physician and patient determine whether a product is worth taking:

1. What is the physiologic basis or theory for this product's action?
2. Are there any scientific studies published in peer-reviewed journals that support or refute the claims that the product makes?
3. Are there any side effects, especially any potentially serious adverse effects?
4. Is the product legal?[4]

TABLE 1
Supplement Costs*

Product	Cost*
Creatine powder	$ 26
Creatine mixture§	60
DHEA	14
Androstenediol	30
Androstenedione	30
HMB	100
Protein powder (50 g daily)	85
Antioxidant formulations	30
Energizing/diet capsules	35
Multivitamins	5 to 20

DHEA = dehydroepiandrosterone; HMB = calcium beta-hydroxy beta-methylbutyrate.

*--Based on a sampling of popular nutrition stores in January 2000 for one month's therapy at lowest usual

Internet

◢ Not only are prohormones potentially dangerous, they are also very expensive. In 1997, Americans spent $11.8 billion on supplements. This amount is expected to increase with time, according to experts.

them for personal consumption. Many bodybuilders and fitness buffs took prohormones on a regular basis.

Due to the 1994 act, the FDA could block the sale of a supplement only after it had determined that the supplement was harmful. Such a determination took a long time. All the while, many new supplements were created. So if the FDA knocked one brand off the market, others popped up to take its place. This problem continues.

Through the 1990s and into the twenty-first century, debates raged about the effects and dangers of prohormones. Proponents say they are not harmful if taken in moderation. Doctors disagree, including Dr. Larry D. Bowers, director of the Athletic Testing

Young athletes need to be aware that there are severe consequences for steroid use. Aside from the physical damage that they may do, a student athlete could be expelled from school or barred from competing.

and Toxicology Laboratory at Indiana University. "We know a lot about that class of drugs," he said. "There's no safe way of taking them, despite what others may say."[2]

The Teenage Epidemic

In recent years, anabolic steroids and performance-enhancing supplements have become more popular among teenagers. Some teens take them to gain a competitive edge. (Though steroids are illegal and banned by sports leagues, enforcement of these rules is not always easy.) Other teenagers take steroids and prohormones to achieve a muscular or "cut" body.

Many prohormones are legal, and as a result, teenagers have easy access to them. Teens also are influenced by muscle magazines, Internet sites, and professional athletes. In 1998, St. Louis Cardinals slugger Mark McGwire admitted to using androstenedione, which was banned by the NFL but not by Major League Baseball. Since "Big Mac" was on his way to seventy home runs that year, young athletes became infatuated with the substance. Said Dr. Lewis G. Maharam, "Athletes aren't listening to their doctors. They're listening to Mark McGwire."[3]

Indeed, sales of androstenedione and other prohormones have skyrocketed since 1998. Meanwhile, such performance enhancers as clenbuterol, HGH, creatine, and ephedra also have been used and abused by many athletes. A 2001 study done by the Healthy Competition Foundation for Blue Cross and Blue Shield Association found that approximately one million young people ages twelve to seventeen had used "potentially dangerous" performance-enhancing supplements.[4]

When Dr. Ziegler developed anabolic steroids in the 1950s, he thought he was creating a wonder drug. He died with deep regrets. "I wish to God I'd never done it," Ziegler said in 1984. "I'd like to go back and take that whole chapter out of my life."[5]

Chapter 3

EFFECTS OF STEROIDS

The first popular brand of steroids, Dianabol, came in the form of tiny pink pills. Today, muscle builders choose from three forms of anabolic steroids: pills, a gel (or cream) that is rubbed on the skin, and a water-soluble form that is injected into the muscle.

In recent years, many users have opted for intramuscular injections rather than consuming pills. "The reason for that is that the side effects associated with the oral form were discovered to be especially worrisome for the liver," said Dr. Gary Wadler, author of the book *Drugs and the Athlete*. "But the injectable steroids aren't free of side effects either. There is no free ride and there is a price to be paid with either form."[1]

▷ Chemical Makeup of Anabolic Steroids

The purpose of anabolic steroids is to imitate the effects of the male hormone testosterone. Testosterone has two effects, androgenic and anabolic. (In fact, the precise term for anabolic steroids is anabolic-androgenic steroids.) Both words have roots in the Greek

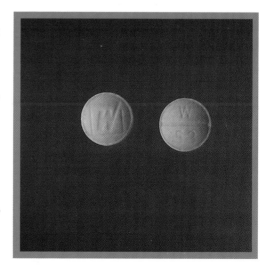

Dianabol was the first popular ▷ steroid. It came as pink pills like Winstrol (shown here), another frequently abused steroid.

language. Androgenic means "masculinizing," while anabolic means "to build."

As a male goes through puberty, testosterone's androgenic effect triggers the maturing of the reproductive system. It also leads to a deeper voice and the growth of body hair. Testosterone's anabolic effect helps the body retain dietary protein, which aids in the development of muscles.

Anabolic steroids mimic both the masculinizing and muscle-building properties of testosterone. Thus, the drugs have several legitimate medical uses. Boys with pituitary malfunctions may that cause them to not grow as fast as other boys may be pre-scribed the drug when they reach the age for puberty.

Men who have their testes surgically removed to rid them-selves of testicular cancer take anabolic steroids. So do adults who suffer from Bells Palsy, a disease that causes people to lose feeling in half of their face. Also, patients who lose muscle tissue—such as AIDS patients or those with certain types of cancer—may be prescribed anabolic steroids. They are also prescribed to patients with anemia, a blood disorder.

However, the vast majority of steroid users have just one goal in mind: building muscle. In fact, scientists have tried to produce steroids that maximize the anabolic effect (for muscle building) and minimize the androgenic effect. What is frightening is that athletes often take a much higher dose of steroids than what is prescribed to patients. Studies show that athletes are taking the equivalent of 20 to 2,000 milligrams (.0007 to .07 ounces) of testosterone per day. That is two to two hundred times a typically prescribed dose.

Steroids' Effects on the Body

Steroid abuse leads to a wide variety of negative side effects. Some of these effects are merely unattractive, while others are life threatening. Some are reversible if the user stops using steroids, but others are not.

Steroid users may pack on more muscle, but it does not mean they are better looking. Steroids can lead to rashes, hives, cysts, extremely bad acne, and oily hair and skin. The drug can cause rapid weight gain and a bloated appearance, which is neither attractive nor healthy.

What is even more threatening is that steroid use increases the risk of atherosclerosis, a condition in which fatty substances are deposited inside arteries. When blood is prevented from reaching the heart, a person could suffer a heart attack. If blood does not reach the brain, one could suffer a stroke. Steroids also increase the risk that blood clots will form in blood vessels, which could lead to heart damage. Numerous steroid abusers, even those in their twenties, have suffered heart attacks and strokes.

Steroids also can wreak havoc on the liver. The drug has been linked with liver cancer as well as peliosis hepatis, a condition in which blood-filled cysts form in the liver. These cysts, as well as the cancerous tumors, can rupture, causing internal bleeding.

The list of side effects goes on and on. Steroids can cause weakened tendons, aching joints, fatigue, and muscle cramps. They can trigger headaches, stomach pain, sleeping problems, trembling, fevers, and vomiting of blood. They can lead to a

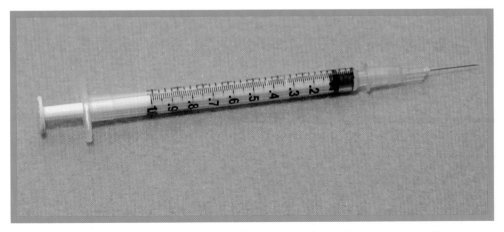

△ Many steroid users prefer to inject the drug into their veins or muscles with a syringe such as this one. People that share syringes are at a very high risk to contract diseases such as AIDS and hepatitis.

decreased sex drive, kidney disorders, and high blood pressure. Consistent use of intravenous needles dramatically increases the risk of infection. Sharing needles could lead to HIV, the virus that can cause AIDS, or other diseases that are transmitted through the blood. Although many of these side effects are reversible, they do not disappear as soon as the user stops taking steroids. Many side effects last a long time after discontinued use.

Men who take steroids to become more masculine can be in for a rude awakening. Steroids can lead to reduced sperm count, impotence, and the shrinking of the testicles. The drug can cause male pattern baldness and gynecomastia—the development of breasts on men. For males, steroids increase the risk of prostate cancer, and they can cause difficulty or pain while urinating. Women who abuse steroids risk becoming more masculine. For females, steroids can cause facial hair growth, a deepened voice, breast reduction, and changes to the menstrual cycle.

Teenagers who abuse steroids risk the above side effects, plus one more. Adolescents who take steroids can suffer from premature physeal closure—also known as stunted growth. "What happens is that steroids close the growth centers in a kid's bones," said Dr. Wadler. "Once these growth plates are closed, they cannot reopen. So adolescents that take too many steroids may end up shorter than they should have been."[2]

▶ Psychological Effects

Anabolic steroids can have an enormous affect on a user's psychological state. Steroids affect the brain's limbic system, which is involved in mood, learning, and memory. The drug is widely known to cause extreme mood swings and aggressive, violent behavior. "Roid rage," in fact, is a phrase that has become part of the sports vocabulary. "I have consulted on several cases where previously non-violent individuals committed murders when under the influence of steroids," said Dr. Harrison Pope.[3]

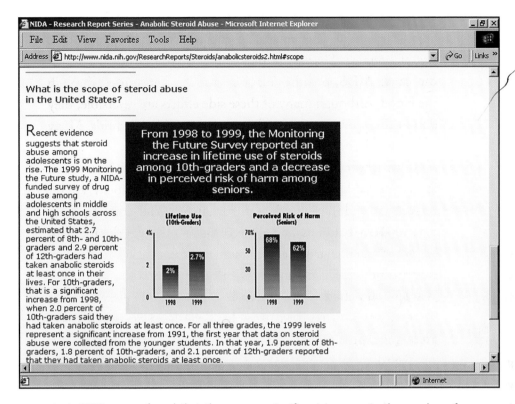

File   Edit   View   Favorites   Tools   Help

Address   http://www.nida.nih.gov/ResearchReports/Steroids/anabolicsteroids2.html#scope

What is the scope of steroid abuse in the United States?

Recent evidence suggests that steroid abuse among adolescents is on the rise. The 1999 Monitoring the Future study, a NIDA-funded survey of drug abuse among adolescents in middle and high schools across the United States, estimated that 2.7 percent of 8th- and 10th-graders and 2.9 percent of 12th-graders had taken anabolic steroids at least once in their lives. For 10th-graders, that is a significant increase from 1998, when 2.0 percent of 10th-graders said they had taken anabolic steroids at least once. For all three grades, the 1999 levels represent a significant increase from 1991, the first year that data on steroid abuse were collected from the younger students. In that year, 1.9 percent of 8th-graders, 1.8 percent of 10th-graders, and 2.1 percent of 12th-graders reported that they had taken anabolic steroids at least once.

From 1998 to 1999, the Monitoring the Future Survey reported an increase in lifetime use of steroids among 10th-graders and a decrease in perceived risk of harm among seniors.

Lifetime Use (10th-Graders)
4% — 1998: 2%, 1999: 2.7%

Perceived Risk of Harm (Seniors)
70% — 1998: 68%, 1999: 62%

▲ *A 1999 survey found that there was a significant increase in the number of tenth graders who had used steroids, as well as an increase in the number of twelfth graders who believed steroids posed a significant risk to their health.*

Some bodybuilders who abused steroids have made the news for their criminal behavior. Bertil Fox, a former Mr. Universe, murdered his girlfriend and her mother. John Riccardi, a California bodybuilder, was also convicted of a double homicide.

Anabolic steroids are not physically addictive, but they can create a mental dependency. Many bodybuilders are afraid to go off steroids. They fear they will become small and weak by losing muscle mass and tone—and thus cannot bear the thought of living steroid free. One study of forty-nine male weight lifters concluded that 57 percent were drug dependent.[4]

Steroids affect users differently. For many, the drugs cause severe depression. Some people even become suicidal. In a 1988

Sports Illustrated article, University of South Carolina lineman Tommy Chaikin described the day he put a .357 Magnum under his chin. "My finger twitched on the trigger," he remembered. "I was in bad shape, very bad shape. From the steroids. It had all come down from the steroids, the crap I'd taken to get big and strong and aggressive so I could play this game that I love."[5]

Stacking and Pyramiding

Some steroid users "stack" the drugs. This means they take two or more different anabolic steroids, sometimes mixing oral pills with steroids they can inject. Users think that a drug combination is more effective than an individual drug, although this has not been proven. Doctors *have* found that combining multiple steroids increases the risk of health problems.

Steroid users may also "pyramid" their doses in cycles of six to twelve weeks. At the beginning of the cycle, the user gradually increases the dosage. In the second half of the cycle, he or she systematically decreases the dosage down to zero. Users feel that the gradual increase allows the body to adjust to the high dosage of steroids. They believe the steroid-free cycle gives the body time to recuperate. The supposed benefits of pyramiding have not been proven either.

Effects of Prohormones

Due to the fact that anabolic steroids are illegal and proven to be dangerous, many athletes in recent years have turned to legal prohormones. Although these are natural supplements, prohormones are similar to anabolic steroids. They aid muscle growth and have frightening side effects.

Many who take prohormones think the supplement must be safe because it is legal. "They have this false sense of security that this has [the] approval of the United States government, because it wouldn't be on the shelves otherwise," said Dr. Wadler. "This is potentially a very serious problem, and it is a sleeping giant."[6]

Androstenedione is the most popular of the numerous types of prohormones. Once consumed, prohormones react with the body's enzymes to produce testosterone. Two hundred milligrams of "andro" is likely to increase circulating testosterone by 200 to 400 percent.

The health risks of prohormones are still being explored. However, studies have found that their side effects seem to mimic those of anabolic steroids. They include acne, irritability, premature balding, lowered HDL cholesterol ("good" cholesterol), and possible kidney and liver damage. Men might experience prostate enlargement, shriveled testicles, breast development, reduced sperm production, and impotence. Among women, prohormones

△ *Pat Bechler, the mother of Steve Bechler (portrait shown), testifies in front of a House of Representatives subcommittee. It was investigating the dangers of ephedra, a product used in over-the-counter weight loss pills, after the baseball pitcher died from complications due to the drug.*

have been linked to disrupted menstrual cycles, facial hair growth, and a deepened voice. Among adolescents, they could lead to stunted growth.

More Dangerous Substances

Besides anabolic steroids and prohormones, athletes take other drugs to improve performance. All are highly dangerous. Clenbuterol is used by European animal trainers to build muscle mass in exhibition livestock. Some bodybuilders think it builds human muscle, too. Clenbuterol, however, can lead to serious cardiovascular complications and is illegal in the United States.

Another steroid alternative is human growth hormone (HGH), which mimics the natural hormone of the same name. Large doses of HGH can cause an enlargement of the face, hands, and feet. It can also lead to heart disease, diabetes, and cancer.

Creatine is an amino acid that some athletes say provides a burst of energy. Medical studies have tied creatine to increased muscle cramping, dizziness, diarrhea, and exacerbation of existing kidney problems. Moreover, the long-term effects of creatine are still undetermined.

Ephedra is an extremely dangerous natural supplement. Athletes take ephedra to lose weight, increase energy, and enhance athletic performance. Yet the FDA has linked ephedra to more than one hundred deaths. On February 17, 2003, Baltimore Orioles pitching prospect Steve Bechler died hours after taking ephedra. Ten days later, Major League Baseball banned the use of ephedra among minor-league players.

Erythropoietin (EPO) is alluring to cyclists and marathoners. EPO increases an athlete's red blood cell count and, hence, his or her stamina. However, it also thickens the blood, making it "the consistency of Jell-O," said Dr. Donald Leggett.[7] This can lead to blood clots, heart attacks, and strokes. The sudden deaths of multiple European cyclists were linked to EPO.

Chapter 4 ▶

HOW STEROIDS ARE PRODUCED AND SOLD

Due to the medical benefits of doctor-prescribed anabolic steroids, pharmaceutical companies continue to produce them. However, far more people seek anabolic steroids to build muscle than to treat ailments. Since such steroids are illegal to buy without a prescription, athletes need to find "underground" sources to purchase them from.

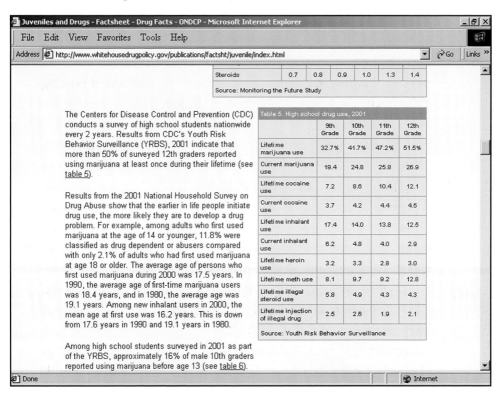

Juveniles and Drugs - Factsheet - Drug Facts - ONDCP - Microsoft Internet Explorer

File   Edit   View   Favorites   Tools   Help

Address http://www.whitehousedrugpolicy.gov/publications/factsht/juvenile/index.html   Go   Links

| Steroids | 0.7 | 0.8 | 0.9 | 1.0 | 1.3 | 1.4 |

Source: Monitoring the Future Study

The Centers for Disease Control and Prevention (CDC) conducts a survey of high school students nationwide every 2 years. Results from CDC's Youth Risk Behavior Surveillance (YRBS), 2001 indicate that more than 50% of surveyed 12th graders reported using marijuana at least once during their lifetime (see table 5).

Results from the 2001 National Household Survey on Drug Abuse show that the earlier in life people initiate drug use, the more likely they are to develop a drug problem. For example, among adults who first used marijuana at the age of 14 or younger, 11.8% were classified as drug dependent or abusers compared with only 2.1% of adults who had first used marijuana at age 18 or older. The average age of persons who first used marijuana during 2000 was 17.5 years. In 1990, the average age of first-time marijuana users was 18.4 years, and in 1980, the average age was 19.1 years. Among new inhalant users in 2000, the mean age at first use was 16.2 years. This is down from 17.6 years in 1990 and 19.1 years in 1980.

Among high school students surveyed in 2001 as part of the YRBS, approximately 16% of male 10th graders reported using marijuana before age 13 (see table 6).

Table 5. High school drug use, 2001

	9th Grade	10th Grade	11th Grade	12th Grade
Lifetime marijuana use	32.7%	41.7%	47.2%	51.5%
Current marijuana use	19.4	24.8	25.8	26.9
Lifetime cocaine use	7.2	8.8	10.4	12.1
Current cocaine use	3.7	4.2	4.4	4.5
Lifetime inhalant use	17.4	14.0	13.8	12.5
Current inhalant use	6.2	4.8	4.0	2.9
Lifetime heroin use	3.2	3.3	2.8	3.0
Lifetime meth use	8.1	9.7	9.2	12.8
Lifetime illegal steroid use	5.8	4.9	4.3	4.3
Lifetime injection of illegal drug	2.5	2.6	1.9	2.1

Source: Youth Risk Behavior Surveillance

Done   Internet

▲ *In 2001, more ninth graders had used steroids at least once in their lifetime than tenth, eleventh, or twelfth graders.*

The Steroid Business

Muscle builders prefer anabolic steroids produced by American pharmaceutical companies because such steroids are regulated and do not contain impurities. Users know exactly what they are getting. However, these steroids are hard to obtain. Pharmaceutical companies track their drugs at every stage of production, making it difficult for someone to steal them.

Moreover, very few doctors will prescribe anabolic steroids for nonmedical purposes. By doing so, they could lose their license and even be arrested. Few pharmacists and hospital workers are willing to risk their jobs by stealing steroids or selling them "under the table." Nevertheless, some "pure" anabolic steroids are stolen and/or wind up on the black market.

Most of the anabolic steroids that athletes use and abuse are manufactured illegally and traded illegally. These steroids are produced in clandestine (secret) laboratories in the United States and other countries—most notably European nations and Mexico. Each year, inspectors at the Mexican border seize hundreds of loads of steroids. The black market for steroids exceeds $400 million a year.

The steroids that are made illegally are not regulated, meaning users have no idea what they are taking. Tablets could contain a smaller dosage than advertised. Worse, the pills could contain a higher dosage, increasing the risks of the drugs. Many of these drugs are fakes, containing no steroids at all. The drugs could be impure, leading to other health risks. Many have included different ingredients than indicated.

Buying Steroids

In every state of the United States, it is illegal to buy anabolic steroids without a prescription. So, how do bodybuilders and athletes get ahold of "the juice?" Often in bodybuilding and sports communities, someone knows someone who has connections.

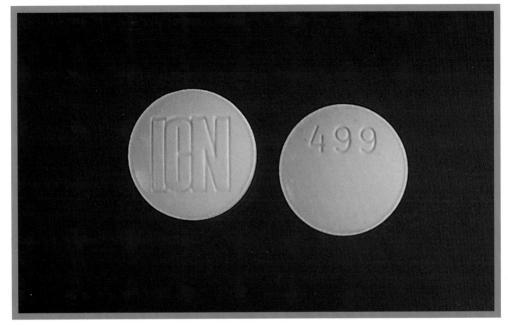

▲ *Android, also known as methyltestosterone, is another well-known steroid. It is illegal to purchase android in the United States.*

Dealers peddle their steroids at gyms, health clubs, training facilities, and even school playing fields. Some bodybuilders that use steroids sell to teenagers, who then sell to their buddies.

In recent years, many users have switched from illegal anabolic steroids to prohormones. These natural supplements are similar to anabolic steroids—in both muscle building and some side effects—but they are legal and easy to obtain. People can buy them at health food stores or through mail-order companies, which are advertised in muscle magazines. More and more, people are purchasing prohormones on the Internet.

▷ Cyberscams

Literally hundreds of companies sell anabolic steroids and prohormones on the Internet. Such sites are so popular that major search engines place frequently visited steroid sites in special highlight boxes. However, buyers should be extremely skeptical of these sites. Many of the site owners are not concerned about their customers' safety. They are interested only in making money.

A large number of these site owners are simply scam artists. Many sites will offer to sell you real anabolic steroids—then take your money via credit card and not send you anything. Or they will send you fakes, which you will not be able to prove unless you hire a chemist to analyze them in a laboratory. Moreover, since you are committing a crime by buying an illegal substance, you cannot complain to the police or to the Better Business Bureau.

Many companies sell dietary supplements on the Internet, including prohormones. Yet many of these companies are dishonest. They will pitch their product as "legal steroids," which is inaccurate. They will glorify the successes of those who have used their product. Many will downplay the risks of prohormones, often claiming there are no "proven" side effects. Supplement manufacturers have even created hip names for their products to entice young people. Names such as Atomic T-Bol, Ripped Fuel, and TestXtreme are meant to appeal to the video-game generation.

Supplement dealers have been known to trick consumers. Many advertise their supplements as prohormones even though they do not build muscle. The FDA has taken several supplement manufacturers to court on charges of fraud—and won.

Some Web sites showcase spokespeople who make big promises, then try to avoid liability with a disclaimer. The disclaimer might say, "The information on this Web site is only that of the author's opinions. This site does not promote or condone the use of anabolic steroids." Such sites are operating just inside the law and should not be trusted.

Penalties for Possessing Steroids

Those who obtain anabolic steroids risk more than just their health. Possession of anabolic steroids is a third-degree felony, and

As of 2004, a first-time offender could face five years in prison and a $250,000 fine for selling steroids. Possession of steroids could also land you jail time.

police take this law seriously. On January 18, 2003, Texas A&M University basketball player Andy Slocum was arrested for possessing anabolic steroids. He was sentenced to ninety days in jail.

People who buy illegal steroids on the internet could wind up in police handcuffs. Think it through: The seller who ships the illegal drug knows not to put a return address on the package. The purchaser's name, of course, is on the package. U.S. Customs workers can seize packages of steroids, and then law enforcement officials will make arrests. The penalty for selling steroids can be as stiff as five years in jail and a $250,000 fine, even for a first-time offender.

Besides risking jail time, athletes can be punished by their teams, sports leagues, or schools. If an athlete is caught using steroids—through a drug test or other evidence—a player can be suspended from his or her team or kicked out of the league. Many schools have strict drug policies that include anabolic steroids as banned substances. Such policies call for the suspension or expulsion of students who use steroids. Many school drug policies state that the school will automatically contact the police if a student possesses an illegal drug.

Though many supplements are legal in the United States, some of them—including androstenedione—are banned by the NCAA. More and more, schools and high school athletic federations are cracking down on the use of supplements. Even politicians are taking a stance. In his State of the Union address on January 20, 2004, President George W. Bush said, "Tonight I call on the team owners, union representatives, coaches, and players to take the lead, to send the right signal, to get tough, and to get rid of steroids now."[1] Members of Congress supported the president's statement with thunderous applause.

Chapter 5 ▶

AVOIDING STEROIDS AND GETTING HELP

Steroids and performance-enhancing supplements, as well as prohormones, are plaguing America's high schools and junior highs. Surveys show that as many as 11 percent of high school athletes have tried anabolic steroids.[1] As mentioned earlier, a 2001 study revealed that a million young people ages twelve to seventeen had used potentially dangerous performance-enhancing supplements. Of this group studied, 96 percent were aware of potential health risks.

▶ Looking for an Edge

For many teens, athletic success is the ultimate glory. Excelling at sports, they believe, will lead to stardom, dates with girls or boys,

▲ Athletes who take the time to learn the correct training techniques and eat a proper diet can gain many of the same edges as athletes who abuse steroids.

scholarship offers, and in some cases million-dollar professional contracts. They will do anything to succeed. The sad truth is that steroids and prohormones no longer give athletes much of an edge.

Not only athletes take steroids and prohormones. Many young people also take them to become more attractive. Males and females want to look "ripped" or "cut." Many sociologists say that young Americans are too preoccupied with obtaining a perfect body. Kids and teens idolize the overly glamorized physiques of athletes, bodybuilders, pro wrestlers, and models. Modern action figure toys boast "six-pack" abs, while pop singers such as Janet Jackson are muscular and lean.

Some athletes and bodybuilders would not juice up on their own but do so because of peer pressure. They figure that everyone else is doing it so they might as well be part of the club. With reinforcement from various sources—muscle magazines, Web sites, and fellow users—athletes feel comfortable taking steroids and prohormones. Unfortunately, this is a false sense of security.

Reasons to Avoid Steroids

When it comes to health, the typical teenager tends to feel invincible. After all, he or she feels healthy, has always been healthy, and doubts he or she will be affected by any "potential" risks of steroids or prohormones. Doctors say this is reckless thinking. As described in Chapter 3, steroids and prohormones can cause a long list of ailments, from acne to heart disease to cancer. They can lead to aggression and depression—roid rage and suicide. Users can be suspended from teams, expelled from school, and locked behind bars.

"Steroid use can induce a spurious sense of hope regarding individual athletic achievement," said Dr. David C. Greenberg, a former team physician for the NBA's Denver Nuggets. "This is quickly dashed when medical problems caused by steroid abuse far exceed any possible performance benefits, real or imagined."[2]

Greenberg said that steroids are particularly dangerous to kids under the age of seventeen. "Even a short period of abusing these drugs could have permanent, damaging effects in this age group," he said.[3]

Adolescents should not avoid just anabolic steroids, but any dietary supplement that promises to improve muscle building, athletic performance, or weight loss. Biochemist Stephen Naylor said it does not matter if the supplement is natural. "Chemistry is chemistry," he said. "Whether you're extracting a hormone from a plant, or chemically synthesizing it . . . it is going to undergo other chemical reactions. . . ."[4] In other words, natural supplements can damage the body, too.

Warning Signs

Steroid and supplement abusers usually try to hide their secret from loved ones. However, they can not hide certain side effects. Keep an eye out for extreme acne or pimples on their face or back, a bloated face or body, rapidly growing muscles, yellow skin, and even bad breath. Note also if they are having trouble sleeping, have a greater appetite, work out more intensely, or are becoming preoccupied with winning. Notice if they exhibit extreme mood swings or uncharacteristically aggressive behavior. These are all signs of steroid use.

Steroid use can lead to violently aggressive behavior. That is just one of the many side effects.

Where to Go for Help

If you or someone you care about has a problem with steroids or supplements, you should discuss it with an adult you can trust. This may be a parent, relative, coach, doctor, or school counselor. In addition, you can contact organizations that aim to help drug abusers. The national steroids hot line is 1–800–STEROIDS. NAADAC, the Association for Addiction Professionals, boasts the nation's largest network of drug-abuse treatment professionals. Other places to contact include the National Drug and Alcohol Treatment Referral Hotline and Narcotics Anonymous.

You can also check your local phone book. It might list a local drug treatment center, a walk-in medical clinic, or a crisis center. You can call your local hospital and ask how they can help you. Help is available, and it is not hard to find.

If you plan to confront a friend or loved one about steroids, it is best to tread lightly. "It is important . . . not to be too aggressive or confrontational at the beginning," said Dr. Harrison Pope. "Many boys and men have become so wrapped up in body image concerns that they almost do not notice it anymore. A gentle, gradual approach from a sympathetic outsider may be the best bet for raising awareness in such a boy or man."[5]

Treatment for Steroid Abuse

Though anabolic steroids are not physically addicting, withdrawal can be difficult. Patients may experience headaches as well as muscle and joint pain. They might also struggle to adjust psychologically; many become clinically depressed. Doctors treat patients differently depending on their condition.

For some patients, supportive therapy is sufficient. They are informed about withdrawal symptoms and are evaluated for suicidal thoughts. If symptoms are severe or long lasting, patients may need to be medicated or hospitalized. They may be

Many former athletes, including Lyle Alzado and Jesse Ventura (shown here), admitted to having used steroids, and later warned people about the ill effects they can cause.

prescribed analgesics for pain or antidepressants for depression. In some cases, doctors prescribe medications to restore the hormonal system. Other patients undergo counseling, cognitive therapy, or psychotherapy.

Alternatives to Steroids

Teenagers do not need anabolic steroids or dietary supplements to become great athletes. After all, the Halls of Fame for every sport are filled with men and women who rose to stardom naturally. Trainers say that the key to success is good instruction, lots of practice, a healthy diet, and proper training. In fact, advanced training techniques—not steroids—are what is hot among athletes. "Today's conditioning experts have their athletes practicing quickness, footwork, speed, and other athletic abilities—physical and mental," said Gary Simmons, a professional athletic trainer and author of *Gymbag Wisdom.*[6]

Before deciding to juice up, think about where the substances are going to take you. Steroids and many prohormones are banned by the NCAA and many professional sports leagues. If you want to improve your looks, consider all the unpleasant side effects of steroids and prohormones: wait gain, acne, hair loss, and so on. A proper diet combined with a good exercise routine is a much smarter alternative.

You may avoid performance-enhancing substances but resent that your teammates and competitors take them. That is a perfectly natural reaction. Discuss the problem with your parents, your coach, or school faculty members. Programs such as ATLAS (Athletes Training & Learning to Avoid Steroids) work with coaches to eliminate steroids and supplement abuse.

Also, do not give in to peer pressure. Many steroid and supplement abusers are not properly educated on the dangers of the products. In fact, they may be "brainwashed" by those who glamorize the substances—be it fellow users, Web sites, or muscle magazines. Educate yourself, and make your own decision.

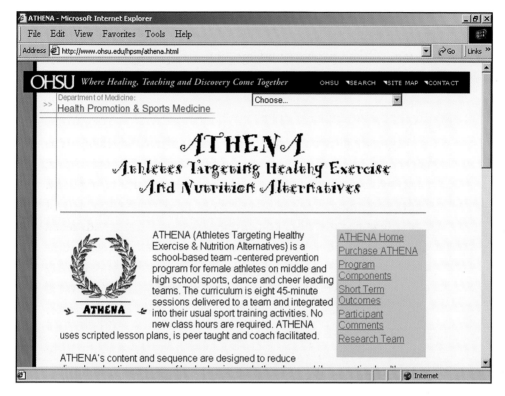

ATHENA - Microsoft Internet Explorer

File Edit View Favorites Tools Help

Address http://www.ohsu.edu/hpsm/athena.html   Go   Links »

OHSU *Where Healing, Teaching and Discovery Come Together*   OHSU   ꜜSEARCH   ꜜSITE MAP   ꜜCONTACT

Department of Medicine:
Health Promotion & Sports Medicine   Choose...

ATHENA
Athletes Targeting Healthy Exercise
And Nutrition Alternatives

ATHENA (Athletes Targeting Healthy Exercise & Nutrition Alternatives) is a school-based team-centered prevention program for female athletes on middle and high school sports, dance and cheer leading teams. The curriculum is eight 45-minute sessions delivered to a team and integrated into their usual sport training activities. No new class hours are required. ATHENA uses scripted lesson plans, is peer taught and coach facilitated.

ATHENA Home
Purchase ATHENA
Program
Components
Short Term
Outcomes
Participant
Comments
Research Team

ATHENA's content and sequence are designed to reduce

Internet

Programs are available to prevent steroid use by teens. ATHENA targets female high school athletes, promoting good nutrition and exercise in an effort to reduce body-shaping drug use and eating disorders.

Aaron is a young man who once abused anabolic steroids, but now he preaches against them. As a football player, he took steroids for five years beginning at age twelve. He developed liver, kidney, and stomach problems, and he was so depressed he tried to kill himself.

Now in his twenties, Aaron tells kids to stay healthy and succeed on their own—not with steroids and supplements. "I took steroids because I did not believe in myself," he said. "I learned the hard way that what matters is how you feel about yourself. . . . What others think fades away, but what you feel inside lasts as long as you live."[7]

anabolic steroid—A man-made hormone derived from testosterone that promotes the building of muscle mass.

androgen—A male sex hormone responsible for the development of male sexual characteristics.

black market—Illegal trade of goods.

cognitive therapy—A treatment approach that focuses on recognizing and changing negative thoughts and beliefs.

cyst—A sac containing gas, fluid, or semi-solid material surrounded by a membrane that develops abnormally in the body.

impotence—A physical state in which a man is unable to engage in sexual intercourse because of his inability to have and maintain an erection.

intramuscular—Into or within a muscle.

intravenous—Into or within a vein.

juice—Slang for anabolic steroids.

limbic system—Interconnecting brain structures that control emotion and memory.

pituitary gland—A gland located in the back of the brain that releases hormones that have an effect on most body functions.

prohormones—A chemical compound that increases the body's supply of hormones.

psychotherapy—Treatment of mental, emotional, and related disorders by psychological means.

roid rage—Aggressive behavior brought on by the use of steroids.

Chapter 1. Frightful Stories

1. "Teen's family sheds light on roid rage,'" August 3, 2001, <http://www.ebcoalition.org/Articals/08-03-01%20Teen's%20family%20sheds%20light%20on%20'roid%20rage'.htm> (September 2, 2003).

2. Kate Randall, "The NFL meat grinder: US pro football player dies in training camp," August 10, 2001, <http://www.wsws.org/articles/2001/aug2001/nfl-a10_prn.shtml> (September 6, 2003).

3. "Steering for Steroids," n.d., <http://whyfiles.org/090doping_sport/5.html> (September 3, 2003).

4. Lance Lahnert, "I made [a] decision and I'm not proud of it," August 27, 2002, <http://www.panhandlesports.com/stories/082702/pig_pp082702-11.shtml> (September 6, 2003).

Chapter 2. History of Steroids

1. "Steroids and Monkey Glands," n.d., <http://216.239.51.104/search?q=cache:gjayZscr2p0J:www.aafla.org/SportsLibrary/IGH/IGH0101/IGH0101k.pdf+steroids+%22medical+dynamite%22&hl=en&start=2&ie=UTF-8> (September 9, 2003).

2. "Androstenedione et al: Nonprescription Steroids," November 1998, <http://www.physsportsmed.com/issues/1998/11nov/news.htm> (September 9, 2003).

3. Ibid.

4. John Meyer, "Added danger," September 15, 2002, <http://www.denverpost.com/Stories/0,1413,36%257E76%257E860245,00.html> (September 14, 2003).

5. Frank Fitzpatrick, "Where steroids were all the rage," n.d., <http://apse.dallasnews.com/contest/2002/writing/over250/over250.features.fourth.html> (September 16, 2003).

Chapter 3. Effects of Steroids

1. "Anabolic steroids," September 6, 2003, <http://espn.go.com/special/s/drugsandsports/steroids.html> (September 18, 2003).

2. Ibid.

3. Cate Baily, "Steroids," n.d., <http://teacher.scholastic.com/scholasticnews/indepth/headsup/drug_steroids.htm> (September 22, 2003).

4. Tommy Chaikin with Rick Telander, "The Nightmare of Steroids," *Sports Illustrated*, October 24, 1988, p. 84.

5. John Meyer, "Added danger," September 15, 2002, <http://www.denverpost.com/Stories/0,1413,36%257E76%257E860245,00.html> (September 14, 2003).

6. "Anabolic steroids," <http://espn.go.com/special/s/drugsandsports/ steroids.html>.

7. Kevin L. Ropp, "Steroid Substitutes, No-Win Situation for Athletes," *Government Publication on Steroids,* 1993, <http://www.timinvermont .com/fitness/govpub.htm> (July 19, 2004).

Chapter 4. How Steroids are Produced and Sold

1. George W. Bush, "State of the Union Address," *The White House,* January 20, 2004, <http://www.whitehouse.gov/news/releases/2004/01/ print/20040120-7.html> (March 19, 2004).

Chapter 5. Avoiding Steroids and Getting Help

1. "Anabolic Steroids and Adolescent Athletes," *American Academy of Family Physicians,* October 1, 1997, <http://www.aafp.org/afp/971001ap/ briefs5.html> (March 1, 2004).

2. Joel R. Cooper, "Anabolic Steroids—Nothing to Get Pumped up About," May 1, 1995, <http://medicalreporter.health.org/tmr0595/ steroid0595.html> (September 29, 2003).

3. Ibid.

4. "Hormones Top Risk List," n.d., <http://www.thomasjmoore .com/pages/dietary_part8.html> (October 4, 2003).

5. "Is Bigger Better?" November 15, 2001, <http://abcnews.go.com/ onair/DailyNews/chat_pope991115.html> (October 1, 2003).

6. "Athletes Don't Need Steroids to Become Great Athletes," December 3, 2002, <http://www.gymbagwisdom.com/pages/press/2002_12_03.html> (October 4, 2003).

7. "Steroids," n.d., <http://library.thinkquest.org/J0112390/steroids.htm? tqskip1=1&tqtime=1201> (October 6, 2003).

Balcavage, Dynise. *Steroids.* Philadelphia: Chelsea House Publishers, 2000.

Bellenir, Ken, ed. *Drug Information for Teens: Health Tips About the Physical and Mental Effects of Substance Abuse.* Detroit: Omnigraphics, 2002.

Connolly, Sean. *Steroids.* Chicago: Heinemann Library, 2000.

Fitzhugh, Karla. *Steroids.* Chicago: Raintree, 2003.

Hinds, Maurene J. *Focus on Body Image: How You Feel About How You Look.* Berkeley Heights, N.J.: Enslow Publishers, Inc., 2002.

Kuhn, Cynthia, Scott Swartzwelder, and Wilkie Wilson. *Just Say Know: Talking with Kids about Drugs and Alcohol.* New York: Norton, W. W. & Company, Inc., 2002.

Marshall, Shelley. *Young, Sober & Free: Experience, Strength, and Hope for Young Adults.* Center City, Minn.: Hazelden, 2003.

Pope, Harrison G., Katherine A. Phillips, and Roberto Olivardia. *The Adonis Complex: How to Identify, Treat and Prevent Body Obsession in Men and Boys.* New York: Simon & Schuster, 2002.

Royston, Angela. *Vitamins and Minerals for a Healthy Body.* Chicago: Heinemann Library, 2003.

Spring, Albert. *Steroids and Your Muscles: The Incredibly Disgusting Story.* New York: The Rosen Publishing Group, Incorporated, 2001.

Taylor, William N. *Anabolic Steroids and the Athlete.* Jefferson, N.J.: McFarland & Company, Inc., 2002.

Phone Numbers

National Steroids Hotline
    1–800–STEROIDS

NAADAC (The Association for Addiction Professionals)
    1–800–548–0497

National Drug and Alcohol Treatment Referral Hotline
    1–800–662–4357

Narcotics Anonymous
    1–818–773–9999